Playground Games

Brighten Up Outdoor Playground Games

Christine Green

Brilliant
PUBLICATIONS

Other Titles in the 100+ Fun Ideas Series:

Practising Modern Foreign Languages
  in the Primary Classroom   978-1-903853-98-6
Art Activities   978-1-905780-33-4
Science Investigations   978-1-905780-35-8
Transition Times   978-1-905780-34-1
Wet Playtimes   978-1-905780-32-7

Published by Brilliant Publications
Unit 10, Sparrow Hall Farm
Edlesborough, Dunstable
Bedfordshire, LU6 2ES, UK
www.brilliantpublications.co.uk

Sales and stock enquiries:
Tel: 01202 712910
Fax: 0845 1309300
E-mail: brilliant@bebc.co.uk
General information enquiries:
Tel: 01525 222292

The name Brilliant Publications and the
logo are registered trademarks.

Written by Christine Green
Illustrated by Cathy Hughes

© Text Christine Green 2009
© Design Brilliant Publications 2009

ISBN 978-1-905780-40-2
First printed and published in the UK in
2009

The right of Christine Green to be
identified as the author of this work has
been asserted by herself in accordance
with the Copyright, Designs and Patents
Act 1988.

Contents

Playground Games

Introduction

Play is possibly one of the first active things children learn in life and so it comes as no surprise to appreciate how fundamentally important such activity is to a child's development. However, when they begin school, play takes on a totally different role, more of a social event as opposed to quality time spent with Mum and/or Dad. It is a time when they begin to integrate with their peers, develop skills and moreover is seen to be an integral part of their overall physical and emotional development.

But it isn't only indoor play that children enjoy and from which they can derive enormous benefits, experts agree that outdoor play is just as important.

■ Play teaches children how to manage some of the risks associated with physical activity.

■ Unstructured physical play is the perfect outlet for helping to reduce stress in a child's life and encourages them to work out any emotional aspects related to everyday experiences.

■ As adults tend not to interfere when children are playing, this in turn enables them to learn how to relax and have fun.

■ Co-operation, helping, sharing and problem solving are all things children learn through play and are skills which they carry with them throughout life.

■ It is very often the case that much of a child's learning is achieved through the media, computers and books etc which, at times, can slightly impede their perceptual abilities. But one shouldn't overlook the other senses, ie touch, taste, smell and the sense of motion via space as being equally crucial to their learning, and this is something which play can provide.

- Research has proven that physical activity not only improves a child's attentiveness and helps to reduce restlessness, but also plays a role in uniting the spirit and body as one.

- And finally, it has been noted that children who are less restricted in their access to the outdoors gain a greater understanding of safety in their immediate surroundings.

Having dealt with explaining why outdoor play is so important to children the next part is providing some games for them to play.

Many of the following games involve the participation of the whole class, others involve only a handful of children and there are several ideas for children to play by themselves. However, one thing they all share in common is to demonstrate to children a healthy fun way of keeping fit and for the teacher the ideal answer for their pupils to use up any surplus energy.

But remember:

- The pupils' safety is important at all times and therefore it is essential that children playing outdoors are always supervised by a responsible adult.

- Accidents can, and all too frequently do occur, even nasty cuts and grazes can result from an over enthusiastic playful push; so if some games become a little too rowdy perhaps this is an indication that a game may not be suitable for them to play and so choose an alternative.

- In order to maintain children's interest and their involvement try to keep the games flowing freely.

Ball games

A ball, whatever its size is primarily one of the most invaluable toys you can provide any child to help them practise rolling, bouncing, dribbling, aiming, throwing, catching, kicking, blocking, and balancing. Throwing helps children learn about accuracy and distance as well as having a lot of fun.

All the ball game activities that are focussed on in this section should be played either on the playing field or on the playground area. Some activities involve the use of extra equipment, ie a skipping rope, stopwatch or whistle, etc., where required, this equipment is listed under the heading for each activity.

For safety purposes, it is always advisable to use a soft ball. For younger children, a larger soft ball may be more appropriate because the ball moves more slowly when thrown, giving the younger child more chance of success.

1. Dodge ball

✦ A favourite ball game for all ages, in particular the older ones.

✦ The concept of the game is for one person to be selected as the 'tagger'. His/her job it is to hit as many people as he/she can with the ball so that they are immediately eliminated from the game.

✦ The winner is the last remaining person who takes on the role of 'tagger' and another game can begin. In order to keep everyone involved those who have been tagged can join in and help catch the others.

Remember: Always use a soft ball. Make it clear that the head and face area must not be aimed at or hit, and that the ball should never be thrown with such force that someone will be hurt.

2. **Team dodge ball**

✦ This variation of Dodge Ball involves the entire class divided into two teams. One team (A) makes a large circle, the other team (B) stand inside.

✦ Whilst team B are running around within the circle, team A have to try and hit one of them with the ball.

✦ But a few rules apply:

◇ Members of team B must not catch the ball otherwise they are out of the game.

◇ Should anyone get hit on the head this does not count and who ever threw the ball is eliminated.

✦ Players who get hit then join the opposing team members.

The winner is the last pupil remaining in the circle.

NOTE – When playing this game with young children have an adult in the outer circle.

Remember: Always use a soft ball. Make it clear that the head and face area must not be aimed at or hit, and that the ball should never be thrown with such force that someone will be hurt.

3. **Dodge ball in threes**

✦ This version of Dodge Ball is ideal for younger children to play in threes.

✦ As in 'Piggy-in-the-middle', two players stand several metres from one another and the third player stands in the middle.

✦ As the two outer children pass the ball to one another they also have to try and hit the child in the middle. However, the person in the middle must try to dodge being hit by the ball, without moving out of their place, so there is a lot of ducking and swaying involved.

✦ Whoever hits the middle person has to change places.

Remember: Always use a soft ball. Make it clear that the head and face area must not be aimed at or hit, and that the ball should never be thrown with such force that someone will be hurt.

4. Zig-zag ball

Equipment: Soft ball; whistle

✦ This game is for older children to play as it can become rather complicated.

✦ The class is divided into two equal teams of seven (A) and (B). They must stand alternately in two parallel lines as shown below:

 Team A

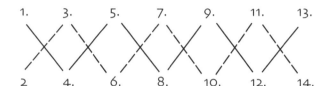

Team B

So members of Team A are numbered 1, 4, 5, 8, 9, 12 and 13 and members of Team B are numbered 2, 3, 6, 7, 10, 11 and 14

✦ When the teacher blows the whistle the basic idea is for the teams to pass the ball in a zig-zag action through their team.
◇ Player 1 throws to player 4
◇ Player 4 throws to player 5
◇ Player 5 throws to player 8 …
… and so on to the end of Team A's line, while another ball is thrown by Team B, 2 to 3, 3 to 6 and so on.

✦ When it reaches the end the ball has then to be thrown back up again:
◇ Player 13 throws to player 12
◇ Player 12 throws to player 9
◇ Player 9 throws to player 8 etc., until it reaches player number one again. Meanwhile, the Team B zig-zags the ball from 14 to 11 to 10, back up to 2.

The winning team is the first to get the ball to one end of their team and back up again but if the ball is dropped at any time that team must start again.

5. **Numbers**

Equipment: Soft ball; pen/paper

✦ One person is designated the thrower. The remaining class members stand together several metres away.

✦ The thrower tosses the ball up towards his/her classmates and then calls out a number between 10 and 100.

✦ An example: Thrower shouts out: '15 up for grabs' and whoever catches the ball is then awarded those 15 points.

✦ The ball is then returned to the thrower.

✦ However, should anyone catch the ball but drop it they lose that number of points – one reason why the teacher should keep a pen and piece of paper to hand.

The winner is the first person to reach 100 points and someone else is then chosen to be thrower for another game.

6. **Score in one!**

Equipment: Length of rope; 4 Large plastic bins; whistle

Throwing helps children learn about accuracy and distance as well as having a lot of fun.

✦ Place a long length of rope on the ground. Several metres behind place four empty dustbins numbered 5, 10, 15 and 20 respectively.

✦ Divide the class into two teams, A and B.

✦ Both teams stand approximately 7 metres from the rope. When the teacher blows the whistle the first member of Team A steps forward, takes the ball and aims at one of the numbered dustbins.

✦ The teacher registers whatever points are scored and it is then the turn of the second player.

✦ After all members of Team A have had a go, it is then the turn of Team B.

✦ At the end of the game all the points are added up and whichever team scored the highest are the winners.

✦ To make it more difficult place the dustbins several metres away from one another.

7. **Target ball**

Equipment: Netball post; chalk

A great playground game and with certain adaptations it is suitable for all ages to play.

✦ Chalk a line approximately 3 metres away from the netball post, then one metre behind mark out another line, continue leaving one metre in between each marking until there are six chalk lines in total.

✦ Each child starts off at the closest mark to the netball post. One by one they must try to throw the ball into the net and each time they succeed are awarded one point and can only then move on to the next chalked line.

✦ If a player misses they must remain on that mark for their next turn and try again. The winner is the first person to reach the last mark and score a goal.

8. Time ball

Equipment: Stopwatch

✦ The basic aim is for each child to individually throw the ball up into the air as high as they can throw. The teacher records the time before it reaches the ground.

✦ Whichever pupil throws the highest (their ball stays up the longest) is the winner.

NOTE: Make sure to choose the area wisely and well away from school windows.

9. **Bridge ball**

✦ Everyone stands in a circle, their legs slightly astride.

✦ One person stands in the middle of the circle. His/her job is to roll the ball through a player's legs. If they are successful that person must then change roles and become the roller.

✦ But what makes the game slightly more difficult is that players must keep their hands on their knees at all times until the moment the ball is rolled. Only then can they try and block the ball from passing through their legs using their hands, but they can't grab hold of the ball, only block it.

✦ The roller can pretend to roll the ball in order to catch someone out, but everyone must be on his or her guard because if they should move their hands before the ball has actually been released they are eliminated from the game.

10. **Catch a theme**

✦   Players all stand in a circle and one person is selected the thrower. He/she has to think of a particular theme, ie colours, weather, capital cities, modes of transport etc. He/she then throws the ball to a player standing in the circle at the same time shouting out the theme upon which the catcher must immediately give an answer within 5 seconds.

Example:
Thrower tosses the ball to a player and shouts out, 'Colour'.
Player catches the ball and immediately has to answer: 'Blue'.

✦   The ball is returned to the thrower.

✦   The thrower then tosses the ball to another player and shouts out 'Weather'. If they reply, snow, rain or sunshine they are still in the game. If the player, thinking it is the same theme as before replies, 'Red', they are out of the game.

✦   It is up to the thrower to decide the theme.

RULES – Players are eliminated from the game if:

   ✧ They can't think of an answer within the 5 seconds
   ✧ They repeat what has already been said
   ✧ They give a wrong answer.

The winner is the last one remaining.

11. **River ball**

Equipment: Chalk; coin

✦ Divide the class into two teams.

✦ Chalk out a long line (riverbank one) and approximately five metres apart chalk out another line (riverbank two). The space in between the lines is the 'stream'. Each team must remain on their own side of the stream at all times.

✦ The teacher tosses a coin to decide which team will have possession of the ball first. The game begins with one player throwing the ball over the stream to an opposing team member who must catch the ball. They must then return it to a different opposing team member and so on.

✦ If the ball falls into the river, the last person who touched it is eliminated and the game starts again.

RULES:

◇ Each time a different person from the team must catch the ball, if the same person catches it twice in a row that team lose a point (minus scores can be used).

◇ If anyone steps into the river to catch the ball they are eliminated.

◇ One point is scored whenever the ball is caught but if it is dropped the person responsible is eliminated from the game.

The winning team is the first to reach 30 points or who have the most remaining team members at the end of the game.

12. Counting down

This is a fun game with no winners or losers and as many or as few children can join in.

✦ Everyone stands in a circle and stretches out their arms so their fingertips are several centimetres free from that of their neighbours. One person begins the game by throwing a ball to the person on their right who then catches it and throws it to their neighbour on the right who in turn throws it to their neighbour on the right and so it continues on around the circle.

✦ But should anyone drop the ball or catch and then drop it they must perform a forfeit chosen by whoever previously threw the ball to them. There are three choices from which to choose:

FORFEITS:

✧ Throw with one hand only

✧ Throw with the opposite hand to the one they would normally use to throw a ball, so if they are right handed they must throw the ball with their left hand and vice versa

✧ Kneel down to throw the ball.

NOTE: Good idea if the teacher stays handy to remind the children of the different forfeits.

Ball games

13. **Danish rounders**

Equipment: 4 cones

Most children are familiar with the traditional game of Rounders played with a bat. However, Danish Rounders only requires a small tennis ball and some cones, (large hoops or even chalked out areas would suffice).

✦ Set the cones evenly spaced apart to create a square and divide the class into two teams, one fielding the other batting.

✦ The bowler bowls a tennis ball under arm to the first batsman.

✦ The batsman uses his/her fist to hit it.

✦ The batsman must try to complete a rounder before the fielding team can throw the ball around each of the four bases and back to the bowler.

✦ RULES:
   ✧ The batsman cannot stop and wait at any of the bases as other players cannot pass him/her and get home until this player has completed his run to fourth base.
   ✧ The fielders have to throw the ball around each of the four bases to reach the fourth base before the batsman to eliminate the player from the game.
   ✧ Players can be run out by a fielder with the ball reaching the base before they do.

When all the team members have had a turn they swap places with the fielders for another match. The team to have won the most points are the winners.

20   *Playground Games*

14. Circle it once

✦ Divide the class up into two teams, A and B.

✦ Team A stands in a circle with one player standing in the middle. Members of Team B have to form a straight line outside of the circle.

✦ A player from team A, stands in the middle of the circle and has to toss the ball to each of his/her team members in turn. and count up the most consecutive catches. If a ball is dropped, they start the count again.

✦ At the same time as he/she is doing this one member from team B must run around the outside of the circle back to their place and tag the next team member who must do the same. This process continues until everyone on team B has run around the circle and returned to their place.

✦ The game stops when all of team B members have completed a run of the circle and returned to their place; it is at this point they have to shout 'Finished'. Then, the thrower from team A has to tell everyone the most consecutive catches his/her team made.

✦ The teams change places for another game and the overall winning team is the one that makes the most number of catches without anyone dropping the ball.

15. **Number hockey**

Equipment: Two hockey sticks; whistle

This is a fast game for playing outdoors on the football pitch and perfect for older children.

✦ Divide the class into two teams. Before the game begins make sure that each team knows the direction of their goalpost. Each opposing team member is given a number and when their numbers are called they must play against one another.

✦ Set the ball in the middle of the playing area with a hockey stick either side.

✦ When the teacher calls out a number whoever has that number from each team has to run out, pick up the hockey stick and try to score a goal for their team. But the fun really begins when the teacher calls out another number perhaps seconds later, so whoever is playing must immediately drop the hockey sticks and change places with the new couple.

✦ On every occasion a goal has been scored the hockey sticks and ball must be returned to the middle of the pitch before a new game can begin. The winning team is the one to have scored the most goals at the end of a five-minute play.

16. **Protect the President**

✦ Players stand in a large circle with two people in the middle. One person is the President, the other person is the Bodyguard.

✦ The other players are given a soft ball and the aim is to try to hit the President but at the same time it is the job of the Bodyguard to stop the ball from hitting him/her.

✦ If at any time the ball touches the President whoever was responsible then becomes the Bodyguard, the Bodyguard becomes the President and the President rejoins the circle.

✦ What makes things more exciting is that the moment the President is hit then everyone must move very quickly as the new President is vulnerable and so the Bodyguard must get into the circle to defend him/her.

A tiring but fun game.

NOTE: Make sure no-one aims the ball at the head or face, if they do they are eliminated from the game.

17. **Spud**

✦ If it is a large class divide them into two teams and one person in each team is chosen to be the 'Potato'.

✦ Potato has to throw a ball as high as they are able into the air and someone else in the group must catch it. The only person who can't catch the ball is Potato. Whoever catches the ball can then throw it up again for another team member to catch and so the game continues.

✦ Each Team has six attempts and whichever scores the highest number of catches is the winner. But there are several rules:

　✧ the same person cannot catch the ball twice

　✧ if someone catches the ball then drops it, they lose a point

　✧ no pushing against one another.

✦ To make it more exciting the teacher could shout out the name of a child to catch the ball and stop any pushing or pulling that may go on.

18. **Kick it once**

Playing area with brick wall
Equipment: Football

Both boys and girls will love to play this game but only play it against a brick wall away from any windows, the only piece of equipment required is a football.

✦ Stand the children in a long line and give the first one a football. Basically the aim is for the ball to be kicked against the wall but as it rebounds the next player in line must attempt to kick it back to the wall followed by the third person in line and so it continues until everyone has had a turn.

✦ Each time they kick it successfully they are awarded a letter that will eventually form the word FOOTBALL.

Kick One – F; kick two – O etc.
If they miss the ball or it doesn't hit against the wall after they kick it then they lose a letter (minus' apply). The winner is the person who manages to get the word FOOTBALL first.

NOTE: Remember to tell the children they have to keep a record of their own letters they score.

19. **Aim and shoot**

Playing area with brick wall
Equipment: Chalk; football

✦ Chalk a large round circle on the wall; this is the target everyone must try to hit.

✦ One by one the children take aim and direct a shot at the target.

✦ Points are awarded:
   ✧ two points for hitting in the centre
   ✧ one point for hitting the circle mark.

✦ Everyone can have two turns and the winner is the one to have scored the highest. If there is more than one winner they play again.

Simple but fun.

20. **Hit or miss**

Playing area with brick wall
Equipment: Chalk; tennis ball

✦ This is a variation of the game above but this time directed towards older children and instead of kicking a football they have to try and hit a tennis ball with their open hand at the target.

✦ Same scoring applies.

21. Stop

This is a game for children of all ages and best played on the field. Even the younger ones will be able to play as long as they listen closely to the instructions.

✦   The teacher selects a child who is given the ball, and whilst the other children run around, that player should toss the ball up in the air and at the same time he/she must call out the name of a class member. The aim is for the person who's name has been called out to try to catch the ball, then shout STOP.

✦   Everyone then has to stand still and the person holding the ball has to choose the person who is closest. They can then take one step towards that person and try to hit them with the ball on their body, arms or legs but not head or face.

✦   If the child misses he/she has another turn and shouts out another name following the same procedure. If he/she hits them, then it is their turn to throw the ball up.

22. **Head catch**

✦ There are some great ball team games and this is one all ages can enjoy playing.

✦ Everyone stands in a large circle with one person in the middle. That person has to throw the ball to anyone in the circle whom they choose and at the same time shout 'catch' or 'head'. The aim is for the recipient to do the opposite to what has been asked of them, so if the thrower shouts catch, then the recipient must head the ball back and vice versa.

✦ The thrower must ensure that the ball is thrown correctly for the ball to be caught or headed.

✦ If the recipient gets it wrong they are out of the game.

28

23. **Caught ball**

✦ One person is chosen to be the thrower and given a tennis ball.

✦ He/she stands facing away several metres from the other pupils. When the teacher gives the signal to throw, he/she has to toss the ball as far as they can backwards over their head at which point the other players have to try and retrieve it.

✦ Whoever gets the ball must shout out 'Caught Ball' and hide the ball behind their back, but everyone else must also put their hands behind their backs. When the thrower turns around he/she has to try to guess who has the ball merely by looking at the expression on their faces.

✦ If the wrong person is identified, whoever did catch it steps forward and becomes the thrower. However, if he/she guesses correctly they can then have another turn and the person who caught it is out of the game.

✦ The winner is the person who manages to stay in as the thrower the longest.

Ball games

24. **Around the World**

Depending on the age of the children either a large soft or small ball can be used in this game. It might be useful to discuss and reinforce topics relating to different countries, ie capital cities, language, currency, famous buildings.

✦   All players form a circle and one person has to stand in the middle with the ball. He/she must then choose a category, ie toys: capital cities, sports etc.

✦   Once decided they must then throw the ball to someone in the circle and at the same time shout out a category to which the person catching the ball has to reply with an answer.
Example:
David throws the ball to Simon and shouts out, 'Capital of France', to which Simon immediately replies, 'Paris' and returns back the ball.

✦   David then throws the ball to another player in the circle and can either stick to capital cities or try to catch that player out and choose another category.

✦   This procedure continues with the ball going backwards and forwards from the centre person around the circle but the person in the middle can throw randomly to anyone.

RULES:

✧   If a player can't think of an answer within five seconds of catching the ball they are out of the game.
✧   If they drop the ball they are out of the game.
✧   If they give a wrong answer they are out of the game.
✧   If anyone repeats an answer already given they are out of the game.
✧   The game continues until all the players are out of the game.

25. **Word ball**

This is a game is very similar to the previous Around the World, but it is intended to reinforce meanings and relations of words.

✦ Explain to the children that you are going to start by saying a word as you throw the ball to the first child.

✦ As this child catches the ball, they will say another word that has the opposite meaning to the word you have just said, for example 'small' … big, large, huge, giant, great, massive etc. See how many words the children can come up with.

✦ Have the children stand in two equal lines opposite each other, while you stand at one end between the lines.

✦ Throw the ball to the first child and say a word (make sure the words you give have plenty of opposite meanings). After that first child has caught the ball, they have to give you an answer and throw the ball to child standing opposite them in the line.

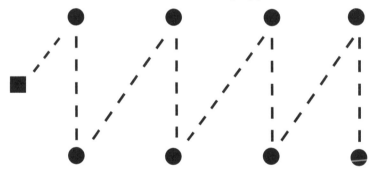

✦ If there is a child who gets stuck, they have to throw the ball back to you and you can either prompt them or give them another 'start' word before throwing the ball back to that child again.

✦ This game can be extended by using word groupings with similar meanings, connections,

26. **Ball rhymes**

Equipment: Soft balls

✦ An old game grandparents would enjoy playing and over the years has undergone many transitions is 'Bumps see daisies' – a game with an accompanying rhyme. In this game the player pats the ball down on the ground continuously, passing it under the leg at the end of each line whilst, at the same time, reciting:

> One two three o'Lairee
> I saw my Aunty Mary
> Sitting on her derriére
> Eating chocolate cake

✦ At the end of the last word 'cake', the person has to bounce the ball hard off the ground and underneath one of their legs, if they miss, it is the turn of another player.

27. Corners

Equipment: Soft ball, chalk

✦ Mark out with the chalk one large square with four smaller squares, one in each corner and a circle in the middle.

✦ Select one child to be 'It' to stand in the centre circle with a soft ball.

✦ All the other children have to stand in one of the four squares. (There can be any number of children in each square.)

✦ The idea of the game, is for you to shout 'Corners'. As you do this all the children in each of the corners have to simultaneously run on to the next corner. (They can only run in one direction.)

✦ While the children are out of their boxes and running, the child in the middle circle has to throw a soft ball at any of the children hoping to hit one of them. If he does so, that child stands out of the box.

✦ The winner is the last one left running.

28. **Hit the bat**

Equipment: Soft ball, cricket/rounders bat or tennis racket for younger children.

✦ Choose one child to start who will bat, all the other childen will field.

✦ The child with the bat throws the ball into the air and hits it with the bat as it falls. He then puts the bat on the ground.

✦ The fielder who retrieves the ball has to throw/roll the ball toward the bat. If he manages to hit it, he becomes the new child to bat.

✦ If someone in the field manages to catch the ball the batter has just hit, then they automatically change places.

29. **Rounders**

Equipment: Soft ball, rounders bat, 4 bases

✦   Divide children into two teams; one to bat and one to field. The batters take it in turn to bat while the fielders defend.

✦   The fielders select a bowler, four basemen, a homebase guard and fielders.

✦   The children hit the ball and score by making a run/rounder by running around all four bases and home again.

✦   Whether or not the batter hits the ball, they can decide to run to first base or further. Each subsequent time the ball is bowled, the runners can move on. They can run on one base or all the way to home base to score a rounder. The batter cannot overtake any of their team members while they are in play.

✦   The aim for the fielding team is to stop as many of their opponents scoring by throwing the ball to any of the bases the opponents are running to.

30. **Bad egg**

Equipment: Soft ball

✦ One player is chosen as the 'bad egg', picks up the soft ball and turns his/her back to the players.

✦ 'Bad egg' then names a category (colours, mammals, planets etc) and then asks the children to name something that falls into that particular category.

✦ Once each child has answered, 'bad egg' calls out one of the answers and throws the ball backwards over his head.

✦ The child that gave this answer does his/her best to catch/ retrieve the ball and then shouts 'stop'.

✦ At the same time all the other children except 'bad egg' run in different directions. At the word stop, they stand still with their legs apart.

✦ The child who has the ball then attempts to throw/roll the ball between someone's legs. If they are successful, the child with their legs apart now becomes the 'bad egg'. If they are unsuccessful, the child with the ball becomes the 'bad egg'.

Rope games

One of the best forms of exercise for all ages is rope jumping and skipping, something that adults as well as children can benefit from. It's an exercise that quickly improves fitness levels, builds self-esteem, and – most importantly – demonstrates that exercise can be fun and enjoyable!

31. Basic skipping fun

Equipment: Stopwatch

Skipping is undoubtedly one of the most popular playground games. With a length of rope both boys and girls can have great fun showing one another their skills and tricks.

✦ Test how many forward skips they can achieve in 30 seconds.

✦ Test how many backward skips they can achieve in 30 seconds.

✦ Count how many skips they can do before tripping on the rope.

✦ See who can do cross over hand skipping.

32. **Blue bells, cockle shells**

✦   Some skipping games have accompanying rhymes many of which contain certain instructions, such as the following one.

✦   Two children hold either end of the rope swinging it back and forwards, but not over and around. At the same time they chant the following rhyme but the skipper must listen very carefully because what they have to do is told in the verse:
Blue bells, cockle shells,
Easy ivy over

✦   On the word OVER the two swinging the rope have to pass the rope once over the Skipper, who must jump, and then continue as they were before swinging it back and forwards.

✦   If the skipper fails to jump over the rope as it comes back down they are eliminated from the game and have to change places with one of the others.

✦   To make it more exciting those swinging the rope can leave out the second line and so only recite the first one several times before saying it.

33. I had a little sports car

✦   Two people at either end turn the rope and, at the same time recite the following:

I had a little sports car,
in 2005, went around the corner
and slams on the brakes.
A policeman came and threw me in jail.
How many days was I there?

✦   The aim of this game is that once certain words are said the skipper has to perform different actions.

✦   Corner – he/she must jump out from the rope, race around the back of one of the turners and return back to the rope again.

✦   How many days was I there? – at this point the two turners have to turn the rope as fast as they can, and the skipper tries to keep skipping while counting.

✦   The skipper is out when he/she messes up with the counting or runs out of energy at which point game one is over and it is the turn of someone else.

✦   Everyone must keep his or her own scores and the one who has reached the highest number is the winner.

34. **Name a Country**

✦ Two people begin swinging the rope at the same time reciting the verse as the skipper is trying to keep up skipping over the rope.

> Banana split with a cherry on the top
> What is the country I forgot?

A,B,C,D,E,F,G,H,I,J,K,L,M,N,O,P,Q,R,S,T,U,V,W,X,Y,Z,

✦ When it comes to the alphabet the two turners can make the rope go fast or slow and then stop at whichever point they want to. At this moment the skipper has 3 seconds to think of a country beginning with that particular letter.

✦ If he/she can't think of a country in 3 seconds they are eliminated from the game and another person has a turn. If they do think of one they can have another go. But if they land on the same letter and repeat the same country again then they are eliminated from the game.

35. **Jack be nimble**

✦ This jump rope game is played with one skipping rope and because it is slightly more difficult is better for older children.

✦ As one skipper takes the rope and begins skipping the other players recite the following:

Jack be Nimble, Jack be quick, Jack leap over the candlestick

Mutter, boot, sizzler, split, pop-ups 10 to 1 HIT it 10,9,8,7,6,5,4,3,2,1.

✦ At the words 'Jack leap over the candlestick', the skipper has to leap up as high as he/she can with both feet leaving the ground at the same time. And when they recite: Mutter, Boot, Sizzler, Split, Pop-ups the following actions must be performed, again by the skipper.

The actions the words represent:
✧ <u>Mutter</u> – put both feet together and make very small hops
✧ <u>Boot</u> – skip while continually kicking one foot outwards and back again
✧ <u>Sizzler</u> – cross and uncross feet and legs
✧ <u>Split</u> – open and close legs approximately five feet apart
✧ <u>Pop- ups</u> - jump off the ground both feet together as high as you can.

✦ To begin with recite the verse slowly. Then when everyone has had a turn speed up the instructions a little, each time getting faster and faster.

✦ The one who was able to perform the most actions when it comes to their turn is the winner.

36. **Red hot**

✦   This is an individual game and as the skipper skips the other players recite:

Red Hot Pepper in the pot
Got to get over what the leader's got.

ACTION: at this point the skipper speeds up the rope and at the same time must count up in fives, ie 5, 10, 15, 20 and only stop when they are tired out.

Keep a record of who achieved the highest score and they are the winner.

37. **Spelling jumps**

✦   One child is chosen to take the rope and spins it around in a big circle.

✦   The rest of the children stand in a circle around the 'spinner'.

✦   Each child takes a turn at jumping the rope as it goes round. Whilst the child is jumping they must spell out a word chosen by the spinner.

✦   When the child has finished spelling their word, they must jump out and let the next child have a turn.

✦   If a child misspells the word, they take over from the spinner.

38. **Two little sparrows**

✦   This skipping game involves four people, two turning the rope and two skippers. The turners recite the following and the skippers have to perform the actions.

   Two little sparrows sitting on the wall.

✦   At this point two players jump in and recite their name.

   One named Stephen, one named Saul.

✦   Each player must wave when his or her name is called.

   Fly away, Stephen, fly away, Saul.

✦   As their name is called the player then has to exit the rope without tripping over.

   Don't you return until your birthday is called.
   "January, February, March …

✦   And the turners go through the calendar.

✦   The player can then return when their birthday is called out.

   Now fly away Stephen, fly away Saul.

✦   Both players leave the rope.

39. **Everyone in**

✦ Several people can play this game, two holding the ropes and three or four people skipping in the middle of the rope. Whilst the two people recite the verse the skippers must follow the actions.

> All in together jump up high.

✦ At this point everyone runs into the rope and begins to skip high

> See if you can touch the sky.

✦ They reach up their hands into the sky

> Everyone blow a kiss.

✦ They have to each blow a kiss

> Everyone has to make a wish.

✦ Close their eyes and make a wish

> Everyone has to shout Hello.

✦ Everyone has to shout out Hello

> Everyone now has to go.

✦ Everyone in the skipping rope has to leave the rope

✦ To make it even more fun start off the rhyme again adding in another person but try keeping the rhythm of the skipping rope going.

40. Alphabet skipping

✦ This is a great skipping game for younger children to join in and at the same time it will help them to remember their alphabet.

✦ Two people swing the rope with an even rhythm and each child has to take it in turns and jump in. As they skip they must recite the alphabet.

✦ If they forget a letter, get it wrong or hesitate then they have to jump out and another person has a turn.

✦ The aim is to get to the letter Z before another skipper can take a turn.

41. **French skipping (1)**

Traditional skipping is performed with pieces of rope, but French skipping is performed using a long piece of elastic or lots of elastic bands tied to one another to form a long loop measuring approximately three metres in length. Initially it can be a little complicated to get the hang of and needs some practice before any competitive games can be played but once the basics have been achieved there are lots of rhymes to chant whilst skipping. Don't attempt the rhymes until you have mastered the steps.

✦ Knot together the elastic bands (see fig 1, page 48).

✦ Two children stand with both ends of the loop positioned around their ankles. They then take one step to the right with one foot, far enough away from each other that the elastic loop is taut (see fig 2, page 48).

✦ The skipper stands in the middle of the loop and then can practice the following jumps:

   ✧ Jump number one – the skipper jumps up and lands with their left foot outside of the loop and the right foot inside (see fig 3).

   ✧ Jump number two - the skipper jumps up and lands with both feet together inside the loop (see fig 4).

   ✧ Jump number three – the skipper jumps and lands with both feet outside the loop (see fig 5).

   ✧ Jump number four – the skipper jumps up and lands sideways to the loop with their left foot on top of the back elastic and the right foot in front of the front elastic (see fig 6).

✦ If the player does not execute the jump correctly then their turn is over and another person has a turn who then must try to get further than the previous player.

Figure 1

Figure 2

Figure 3

Figure 4

Figure 5

Figure 6

Playground Games

42. **French skipping (2)**

A slightly more difficult variation from the previous page.

✦ You need a minimum of three players, two players standing inside the loop so they are stretching it taut around their ankles. The job of the third player is to perform a number of jumps making sure that after each move their feet land in specified positions in relation to the gaps of elastic between each player as such.

1) Both feet under the elastic
2) Both feet on top of the elastic
3) One foot on top, one foot underneath
4) One foot on top, one underneath then change feet quickly before moving to the next stretch of elastic (known in the game as 'swapsies').

✦ Once the round of jumps has been successfully completed at ankle level, the height of the loop should be raised by 10 centimetres increasing the difficulty of the jumps.

✦ Should however, the current skipper not undertake the correct jump their turn is over and play would transfer to one of the other players who would then try to get further than the previous player.

43. Back-to-back skipping

✦ Four people are required to play this game. Two people take either end of the rope and begin to swing it whilst the other two people stand inside the skipping rope back to back.

✦ The two swinging the rope, (it can be passed overhead) say the following lines whilst the two skippers must listen carefully and follow the instructions.

✦ Back-to-back (they must keep back to back whilst still jumping).

✦ Face-to-face (they must quickly turn around, at the same time keeping up with the skipping).

✦ Shake your partners hand (they must shake hands with one another, still jumping).

✦ Change place (this is the tricky one where they have to swap places, again still jumping).

✦ If either skipper fails to follow the actions then they change places with one of the turners and another game can start. The fun is in seeing who has the longest turn skipping.

44. **Postman, Postman**

✦ This game is designed for two people to play. Whoever has charge of the skipping rope has to sing whilst the other person has to be ready to jump in when their part is sung.

> Postman Postman do your duty
> Here comes (at this point he/she calls out the name of the other skipper who has to jump in)
>
> Katie, the English beauty.
> She can wiggle, she can waddle, she can do the splits.
>
> She wears her dresses (at this point the singer can choose between one of the following: around, below) her hips.

✦ When her hips or whatever other part of her body the singer chooses is sung the second skipper must pretend that she is putting on a dress and still keep skipping at the same time.

45. Your Royalty

✦ This rope game is a combination of Follow the Leader, Tag and Jump Rope.

✦ The idea is that two people keep on twirling the rope whilst two other people have to skip, one is Your Royalty and the other skipper is the Worker.

✦ Whatever action Your Royalty performs, it might be to hop or clap their hands, move further down the rope or even jump out of the rope, the Worker must do exactly the same, and, at the same time try to catch and tag them.

✦ The only way, other than tagging, the Worker can be eliminated from the game is if they copy their master and shout out I'm King/Queen. So imagine the chaos in trying to tag someone, at the same time concentrating to do whatever action they are doing but remembering not to shout out – it is not easy.

✦ Only when the Worker has managed to tag 'Your Royalty' can they change roles.

✦ To make it even more fun you could play the game with four people always making sure they follow their master.

Some actions for Your Royalty to try:

✧ Hop on one leg then change to the other

✧ Clap their hands in the air then down at the ground

✧ Spin around after jumping over the rope

✧ Run out of the rope, go behind one of the turners and come in at the opposite direction

✧ Shout out I'm King/Queen.

46. **Tug of War**

Extra Equipment: Chalk

✦ A super challenging team game. Divide the class into two teams but try not to make it boys against girls. A long piece of rope is stretched out across a chalked dividing line on the playground.

✦ After the count of three the teacher gives the signal and both teams start pulling towards their direction. Whichever team manages to pull the other team over to their side are the clear winners.

47. **Banana split**

✦ This game requires a long rope and a group of children perhaps four or five.

✦ The jumpers all form one line parallel to the rope. Each turner turns the rope once towards the line of jumpers, and then one turn away from them.

✦ The trick is that the jumper must not jump over the rope but run underneath it, and so, as the rope is reversed they come back underneath it never allowing the rope to touch them.

✦ After the first jumper has had a go they repeat it again but this time another child accompanies them so it is two going under the rope and then passing back through again.

✦ Should anyone miss or touch the rope the game is over.

48. Bring them in

✦ This is a fun game and all it requires is a long rope and a number of children. The skippers form one line to enter the rope near one of the turners. With each turn of the rope another skipper is added but they must huddle up close each time to make room for another one to join.

✦ If anyone misses their turn, or touches the rope the game is over.

49. Catch me

✦ This is a challenging game that everyone will enjoy furthermore; it helps to develop concentration, turning skills and endurance in the children.

✦ This game involves three children and one long rope per group. As two children turn either end of the rope the third child has to jump inside anywhere they wish to and the turners have to keep the momentum of the skipping rope up.

✦ The turners have to try and get the skipper out so they can turn the rope slow then speed up whenever they want to and as long as the skipper keeps up with them they can remain in the game. Once they stumble they are out of the game and it is then one of the turners chance.

50. Figure ropes

✦ This is a fun game to play for all ages. Simply divide the class into groups and supply each one with a rope. Give them three minutes to make up a fun figure using the rope and then see who can guess what each others shape is supposed to be.

51. **Walk tall**

✦ The ideal rope game, which can be played indoors or outdoors. Place the rope in a straight line on the ground.

✦ The aim of each player is to try to walk the straight line, holding out their arms to balance as they walk. It may sound easy but requires a lot of concentration and if they should lose balance at any point then they are out of the game, whoever reaches the end without falling is the winner.

52. **Walk the rope**

Equipment: Blindfold

✦ A variation on Walk Tall but on this occasion the class is split into three teams depending on how many students are in the class. Each team is given a rope that they place on the ground (grass may be safer in case anyone falls) in a zig zag design.

✦ One person is blindfolded and another team member, preferably the one whose turn it is next must give their player instructions on how to walk alone the rope to the other end (you could ask them to come back again, but this depends on time available).

✦ If the player falls off or gets it wrong they must go back to the beginning and start again. Once they have completed the walk in both directions they can remove the blindfold and it is the turn of the next member to walk the rope and the next person in line after him/her to guide their team member.

✦ The first team to have all members successfully completing the walk and back to their place are the winners.

53. **Down by the River**

✦ Another skipping chant for counting practise

Down by the river, down by the sea
Johnny broke a bottle and blamed it on me.
I told Ma, Ma told Pa,
Johnny got a spanking, ha, ha, ha.
How many spankings did Johnny get?
One, two, three, four … and so on

✦ Keep counting until the child lapses. You could give out stickers for the highest number of jumps.

54. Find the knot

✦ Using two lengths of rope, knot the ends together to form a loop.

✦ Everyone has to stand in a circle holding up the rope. Slowly each player passes the rope around the circle, trying to disguise where the knots are.

✦ One person, chosen randomly by the teacher, must stand in the centre of the circle and when the teacher shouts stop he/she must then try to guess which player is holding a knot in their hand.

✦ If they guess correctly they change places. If wrong the game continues until a correct guess is made.

55. Getting under

Be prepared for a lot of giggling with this game.

✦ Show the children how to limbo.

✦ Two people stand at either end of a length of rope with it held taut at a certain height.

✦ Taking turns, each member of the class must try to limbo under the rope without touching the ground or rope in any way. When everyone has done it successfully the first time, the rope is slightly lowered again and this continues until everyone is out of the game.

✦ The winner is the one who can successfully limbo under the rope without falling, touching the ground or the rope.

56. Ropes in the waistband

✦ An exciting game to play where short pieces of rope are required.

✦ Each pupil tucks a small piece of rope into their waistband but leaves at least 30cm showing.

✦ When the teacher shouts 'Go' everyone must try to catch one another and pull each other's rope from their waistband. Whoever loses their rope is out of the game.

✦ The winner is the last remaining player who still has their rope.

57. **Teddy Bear**

✦ Two people hold the skipping rope and turn it over.

✦ The children take it in turns to jump in and complete the actions that the turners are singing in this rhyme:

Teddy Bear, Teddy Bear, turn around,
Teddy Bear, Teddy Bear, touch the ground
Teddy Bear, Teddy Bear, show your shoe
Teddy Bear, Teddy Bear, that will do!

58. **Changing places**

✦ The children form a circle around two children turning a skipping rope.

One elected child jumps in as the rope is turning and chants the rhyme below:

I like coffee, I like tea,
I'd like (person's name) to jump with me.

✦ That person joins the first person so that two are now jumping. The rope turners then count the number of jumps they make, saying them out loud. Once they get to ten, the first of the jumping pair must leave.
One, two, three, four, five, six, seven, eight, nine, ten, time to move on and start again.

The first child jumping must jump out leaving the second child to start the chant again and call in another to jump.

Running games

Children run all the time. It is a great way for them to exercise and burn off surplus energy. And what better way when at school to combine both the educational and entertainment element that running provides than partaking in some playground running games.

These games combine taking part both as individuals and as members of a team, encouraging the children to build on their interactive and co-operative skills.

59. **Hop, skip and jump race**

Equipment: Two cones; several bean bags (one for each pupil)

Relay races that several children in the class can play together are always popular and this one is ideal for all ages to play.

✦   The teacher distributes beanbags (enough for each pupil in each team) beside the cones that are placed a 'measured' distance from the start line.

✦   The children line up in teams at the start line and on the signal 'Go' the first child from each team has to hop up to the end of the track go around the cone, pick up a bean bag and hop all the way back to the beginning. Only when they tag can the next player start and they must ship to pick up their beanbag. And the third player tagged must jump up the course to pick up their beanbag.

The team who are first to complete all the movements on the course collecting all the beanbags are the winners.

60. **Windows and doors**

This is a slightly competitive and certainly exciting game for children.

✦   Players form a circle, and then stretch out their arms making sure they just touch their partners' fingertips, creating large spaces in between one another. These are called the windows and doors.

✦   One child starts running, weaving their way in and out between the children's arms and as they pass through anyone can randomly drop their arms and try to touch the person weaving their way in and out.

✦   Once that person is touched they are immediately out of the game and another person is chosen to start off weaving in and out through the windows and doors.

✦   The winner is the one who is able to pass through the circle and return to their place without being touched. The game becomes more difficult as less people are left playing.

61. **Human chain**

Lots of energy is used up in this fun game.

+ Whilst two people are chosen to play the role of captors the rest of the class can run around freely.

+ The game begins when the two chosen captors hold hands and set off chasing after someone to join their chain. Whoever they catch then becomes another member and so joins in the human chain by linking hands, and off they go again in pursuit of another victim.

+ After the second person is caught it is up to the main captors to decide whether they split into pairs or stick together as four. However, they can only split off when they have even numbers. The game continues until everyone has been caught into a human chain.

62. **Scream!**

Be aware this is a noisy game and so should preferably be played on a large open field well away from the rest of the school.

+ Everyone lines up alongside one another at one end of the field, and as the teacher shouts 'Now' each child takes a big breath and screams as loud as they are able, whilst running towards the opposite side of the field.

+ It may sound easy but the trick is that they can only run for as long as they can scream, so when they run out of breath they must stop.

+ Whoever runs the farthest is the winner.

63. Relays

Possibly the one main attraction in playing relays is that it helps build up a child's stamina as well as offering other types of exercise. They also give confidence to many children who are scared of standing out in a crowd simply because there is never just one winner or loser it is a joint effort. There are lots of fun variations in the relay race, perhaps you may like to give the following a go!

✦   Big Foot Relay. Each team has an extra large sized pair of wellies that they have to put on, race up to a cone and back again before taking them off for the next team member.

✦   Cup Stack Relay. Stack up two sets of 6 plastic cups on trays a distance away. First set of runners have to run up, unstack the cups and run back, next set of runners have to run up and re-stack the cups before returning and so on.

✦   Ball and Cone Relay. Set up four cones for each team with a tennis ball balanced on each of the first three. The team players have to pick up the ball from cone three and place it on cone four and run back. The second player the has to pick up the ball from cone two, put it on cone three, run around cone four and home. The third player has to place the ball from cone one onto cone two, run to the end around cone four and home. Finally player four has to run up to cone four, bring back the tennis ball and place it on cone one again and cross over the line.

The teacher should decide on the running distances. Take into account the ages of the children and the time you have available.

64. **Running over hurdles**

Equipment: Three or four cones; bean bags; collapsible cardboard boxes; pieces of cane with rounded ends

✦   Children are divided into teams of three or four and a cone is placed at the beginning of each group. Obstacles such as beanbags or boxes that are collapsible, perhaps a cane with tapered ends balanced across two cans, so if they get knocked over the children can't hurt themselves, should be placed around the playing field.

✦   At the word, 'Go', the first child from each team must run over each obstacle without knocking it down and then sprint back to their place slowing down to move around the cone behind the team and touch the next person on the shoulder who should then run off as fast as they are able to.

✦   If you want to make the game slightly more difficult for older children increase the distance between the hurdles and/or increase the height of the hurdles.

✦   Whichever team are the first to finish are the winners.

NOTE: Make sure that the obstacles the children are running over are capable of collapsing safely when hit. All the children should run in the same direction and may need to be shown by the teacher. If canes are used do make sure the ends are tapered.

65. Ice-cream shop

✦ The children stand in a circle with one chosen to be in the middle. He/she is the shopkeeper.

✦ All the children in the circle are given an ice cream flavour, ie chocolate, vanilla, strawberry and chocolate chipped (choose about four). The shopkeeper calls out a flavour and whoever has that particular flavour runs to the other side of the circle. But if they are tagged by the shopkeeper they must stop exactly where they are and become shop assistants and have to help tag people but they are not allowed to move from where they are standing.

✦ The last one to be caught takes on the role of Shopkeeper for the next game.

✦ You could make it more exciting by calling out a number of flavours together or to make it even more exciting call out Ice Cream shop in that case everyone has to run to the other side of the circle.

66. **Handless ball race**

Equipment: Pen; paper; small ball; small bowl

✦   Some preparation is required by the teacher beforehand. Copy down the rules on pieces of paper, one rule for each participant, if there are more than eight players just duplicate some of the rules. Fold up each slip of paper and pop it into a bowl.

✦   This hectic game is best played with eight or more players.

✦   Divide the players into two equal teams and stand them in a straight line. One player from each team must reach into the bowl and pull out a piece of paper with an instruction written on it.
Rules:
1) You cannot use your hands.
2) You must use only your arms.
3) You must not let the ball touch the ground at any time.
4) You can only use your fists.

✦   The aim of the game is for a ball to be picked up from the ground and transferred from person to person through the team and back to the first person again following the instruction written on the paper.

✦   The teams both have 60 seconds in order to read the slip of paper and discuss what they think is the best way of carrying out their instruction. When the 60 seconds is up the game starts and whichever team completes the task successfully and returns the ball to the first person are the winners of that round and another game can commence.

NOTE: If any of the rules are broken the ball must be returned to the beginning of the line to start again.

67. **Where's my shoe?**

Equipment: Players shoes/plimsolls

✦ This game should be played preferably on a warm summer day and outdoors on a large field.

✦ It requires five girls and five boys who must remove their shoes (or plimsolls, sports shoes).

✦ The teacher marks out two lines 10 metres apart. At the second line the children pile up their shoes and return to the start/finish line.

✦ When the teacher says 'Go' the players have to run up to the line, find their shoes, put them back on and return back to their team. The next person in line then repeats the process.

✦ The first team to each have a turn and be sitting in a straight line with their shoes fastened are the winners.

68. Hens and chicks

Equipment: Chalk

This is an ideal game for very young children to play.

✦ Chalk out two round circles on the playground approximately 15 metres apart.

✦ One pupil is chosen to be Mother Hen who must stand in between the two circles. The remainder of the class are then divided into two groups, one team standing in each of the two designated circles.

✦ When Mother Hen shouts 'Come Home Chickens' each group have to swop locations while 'Mother Hen' has to try and catch as many 'Chickens' as she can.

✦ Whoever is caught must then remain and help Mother Hen. The last chicken caught gets to be the next Mother Hen.

69. Where's the sock?

Equipment: Sock

✦ This game can also be played indoors but is just as much fun played outdoors when the weather is warm and is particularly suitable for younger children.

✦ A nominated pupil takes the role of the shopkeeper. He/she places a sock on the ground behind them and then stands with their back facing the rest of the group. They are all standing around in the crowd facing the shopkeeper's back.

✦ The teacher quietly points to one player who must very quietly sneak up behind the shopkeeper, pick up the sock, run back to their place in the crowd and hide it somewhere on their body, it could be up the back of their jumper, or worn on a hand, stuffed up their sleeve or even hidden in between their legs. The fun bit begins when the children all chant:
    Shopkeeper, shopkeeper where's your sock,
    Has someone stolen it from your shop?

✦ The shopkeeper then turns around and has to try to guess, from the look on the faces or other means who may be responsible. He/she can take three turns at trying to guess the identity and if they are right then they can take another turn but if they get it wrong whoever has the sock becomes the shopkeeper and another game can begin.

NOTE: Try and tell the players to keep as straight a face as they can otherwise they will give the game away.

70. Chicken, Chicken

✦ All players sit down in a circle facing one another. One child is nominated the Farmer who walks around the outer part of the circle.

✦ As the Farmer walks around he taps people randomly on the shoulder and tells them they are a Chicken. That person must immediately jump up and chase the Farmer around the circle before he/she is able to return to the Chicken's spot.

✦ If the Farmer wins then the chicken must sit in the circle and wait there until another chicken has a turn and beats the Farmer in which case the Chicken is free to return home. If the Farmer wins that chicken must also join his/her friend in the circle.

✦ Should the Farmer get tagged by the Chicken then the Chicken becomes the Farmer and the Farmer must sit down in the middle and can only leave when another player joins them.

71. Freeze

✦ This is another version of the popular game Tag in which one person is still 'it' but when they touch someone, then whoever it was must immediately stand still. The only way they can be freed is if someone crawls between their legs. The game continues until all the players are standing in statues and the last person to be tagged is 'it' for the following game.

72. Nudge, nudge

This game is great fun for young children to play outdoors and use up their excess energy.

✦ Everyone runs around freely but as soon as the teacher shouts 'Shoulders' the children must pair up immediately with someone and touch the other persons' shoulders.

✦ The second round begins again with the children running around but this time the teacher shouts out another part of the body, perhaps 'Elbows', at which point the children have to pair up again, but this time with a different partner and touch their elbows.

RULES – Players are eliminated from the game:

✧ If anyone can't find a partner they are out of the game.

✧ If they go to the same person as before.

73. **What number are you?**

✦   This is a good game, not only is it fun to play but it also has an element of education by helping young children learn to count.

✦   The children run around the playground until the teacher shouts out a number no less than 2 and no more than the number of children in the class.

✦   When the teacher shouts out a number, ie four, the children must get themselves into groups of four. And the game just continues with the groups dispersing playing around for a while until the teacher calls out another number and the children have 30 seconds to get themselves into that numbered group. Any who fail to join a group within the time are out of the game.

✦   Obviously as less and less children play the numbers shouted will have to be reduced.

74. **Take it steady!**

Equipment: Bean bags; cones

✦   Children are divided into two teams and each team is given a beanbag.

✦   The teacher marks out a designated spot with a cone several metres from where the children have formed a line.

✦   Both teams line up one behind the other and the object is for each member, one at a time, to walk to where their cone is located with the beanbag balanced on their head. When they reach their respective cones they have to return to their team members doing whatever action the teacher requests on this occasion, still with the bean bag balanced on their head, ie hop, run, or skip. Only when they reach the next player in their team can that next player go.

75. **Anti-litter**

Equipment: Waste-paper bins, empty yogurt cartons

✦   Divide the children into four or five teams with equal numbers
.

✦   Mark out a circle of about three metres in diameter. Put a pile of empty yogurt cartons in the centre.

✦   At equal distances from the centre circle, place the waste-paper bins.

✦   Get the teams to line up one behind the other behind their bin. On the starting cue, one child from each team runs to the centre circle, picks up a yogurt carton, returns and puts it in the waste-paper bin.

✦   At the moment the carton goes into the bin, the next team player may start.

✦   The game ends when there are no more cartons to collect and the winner is the team to have collected the most cartons.

76. **Speed running**

Equipment: Chalk; stopwatch; cone

✦ A game guaranteed to make children appreciate the joys of fast running, to work in pairs and also have a better understanding of time and distance.

✦ Divide the class up into pairs and chalk a line on the playground that all pairs must stand behind.

✦ One player takes a cone (or similar piece of equipment) and places it at a distance that their partner says they are able to reach within a time limit of five seconds. They are then given a stopwatch to record the time.

✦ At the signal 'Go', the runner must try to reach the cone or at least as far as they are able to until their partner shouts 'STOP'. Their partner then puts a mark where they were able to each.

✦ Re-position the cone and try again, hopefully this time the runner may reach the cone and beyond in that five second limit.

✦ Then change over roles so the partner becomes the runner and vice versa.

✦ There are no real winners or losers but for a play off they can ask a classmate to time them both for five seconds when they both race against one another to see who goes the furthest.

77. **How many sides?**

Equipment: Cones or wall

✦ Revise with the children the names of different shapes and how many sides they have.

✦ Have the children stand in a line, a short distance from a line of cones or a wall.

✦ Select a child and ask them to tell you how many sides a particular shape has.

✦ Tell the rest of the childen if they agree, they should race to the wall and back again.

78. **Find the sweet**

Equipment: Bowl, sawdust, sweets in wrappers

You can use this as an individuals game or a team effort.

✦ Hide a sweet in a bowl containing a small amount of sawdust. Place the bowls a certain distance from where your start line will be.

✦ Instruct the children to race to the bowl, find the concealed sweet and run back to the finish line.

✦ Have the children stand on a start line and blow your whistle or shout 'Go'.

✦ If you are going to run this game with teams of players, then you will need to hide several lots of sweets in each bowl of sawdust.

Group Games

The games in this section are for groups or teams. They are primarily designed for everybody participating to have fun and enjoy themselves. These games also help children develop the fundamental social skills needed throughout life. They will help build self-confidence, increase their level of co-operation and awareness not just in themselves but in each other.

79. Red letter

✦ One person is chosen to be the leader.

✦ He/she stands approximately 2–3 metres away from the rest of the players with their back towards the others and calls out a letter of the alphabet. If any players' first name contains that letter they can move forward (one step per letter) towards the leader, the number of steps he/she takes depend on how many letters they have in their first name.

✦ Take for example, if the letter 'A' is called out and someone in the group is called Marie then she can take one step forward because there is only one letter 'A' in her name. However, if another child is called Adam, then because there are two 'A's in his name he can take two steps forward.

✦ The leader continues calling out letters until someone reaches them and taps them on the shoulder. It is then their turn to become the leader.

REMEMBER: No letter can be repeated twice and if the caller turns around they are out of the game and someone else must take over.

For older children, the letters could be chosen out of a bag to avoid the leader picking the letters in a friends name.

80. Bring back the gloves

Equipment: Chalk, glove or beanbag; 2 blindfolds

✦　　A chalked line is drawn down the centre of the playground and the class divided up into two teams.

✦　　Each team stands on opposite sides of the line and are given a number with a corresponding player having the same number.

✦　　The teacher places the glove in the middle of the chalked line and then calls out a number, ie number two and whichever players share that number must step forward. They are then allowed to have a few seconds to look and remember where the glove/bean bag has been placed and then they are blindfolded.

✦　　This is the tricky part because they have 10 seconds to try and remember where the object they have to retrieve was located without any help from their team members shouting out. When the teacher says, 'Bring Back the Glove' the first player to pick up the glove and return it to their 'home side' is the winner and their team awarded one point.

✦　　If after the ten seconds is up, neither player has found the glove, it is the turn of another pair to have a go and whichever player is eventually successful, that team is awarded two points.

RULES:

   ✧　　No players from either side are allowed to shout out.

   ✧　　No peeping out from the blindfold.

81. Under the arches

✦ You need at least ten people to play this game, but the more the merrier.

✦ Everyone stands in a circle, holding hands with their arms raised to create a series of arches. One person is chosen who must run in and out of the arches. At the same time the rest of the pupils sing:

> In and out the yellow daisies
> In and out the yellow daisies
> In and out the yellow daisies
> I am your captor.

✦ At this point the person who has been 'trying to escape' stops behind a member of the circle and starts to pat them on the shoulder and sing:

> Pitty Pitty Pat Pat on his/her shoulder
> Pitty Pitty Pat Pat on his/her shoulder
> Pitty Pitty Pat pat on his/her shoulder
> I am your captor

✦ After singing this song that person must now move out of the circle and go behind the runner and, holding on to his/ her waist they both now have to run in and out of the arches. Again the rest of the group begin singing:

> In and out the yellow daisies
> In and out the yellow daisies
> In and out the yellow daisies
> I am your captor.

✦ This goes on until the chain gets longer and longer and there is no one else remaining in the circle. Great fun and a good way to use up excess energy.

82. Pilchards

✦ Younger children will enjoy playing this game that is very much like a game of hide and seek but on this occasion only one person hides and the rest have to try to find them.

✦ As everyone stands huddled together in a group, eyes tightly shut, the teacher taps one pupil on the shoulder who must find somewhere within the school grounds to hide. Everyone else counts to twenty after which time the teacher pairs pupils off who must try to find that person.

✦ The pair to find him/her are the winner and the group reassemble back together again for another game when the teacher chooses another pupil.

83. Who's the Donkey?

Equipment: Tennis ball

✦ The children stand in a circle several metres apart.

✦ The idea is that the ball is passed between the pupils until it is dropped. As soon as the ball starts being passed around the circle the children begin counting from 10, 9, 8, 7, 6, 5, 4, 3, 2, 1, 0 and the last person to have touched the ball at '0' becomes the donkey.

✦ Depending on the time-scale allow each person two/three lives. The game continues until there is only one person remaining who is the winner.

84. Fishes in the Sea

✦ For this game there has to be at least 3 players. There are two lines at a distance from one another. In between the Shark lies in wait to capture all the small fish that are standing behind the line. They must try to get over the second line without being caught by the Shark.

✦ The fish must call out this small verse:
> The Fish in the Red Sea,
> Which colour must we have to get to the other side?

✦ At this point the Shark must have his/her back turned to them and call out a colour, ie red. All the fish who are wearing something red or has this colour on their clothing, it could even be a colour in their shoelaces, can walk over without being afraid of being caught by the Shark. But those who do not have the colour red on their person have to go very carefully because they are the ones that the Shark can catch.

✦ Safety waits for all the fish over the second line but those captured become the Shark's helper. The next round continues with the Shark choosing another colour and this time there is a greater chance of more fish being caught because there are more helpers. They have to run back and forth as fast as they can until all the fish have been caught and the one to avoid being captured is the winner who now becomes the Shark in a new game.

85. One legged

Equipment: Chalk

✦ The class is divided into two teams of equal numbers.

✦ One group are the rabbits. The other group are the players. Three large chalked circles are drawn on the playground – one for the rabbits, one for the players and the third one for prisoners.

✦ The players have to all remain in their circle, whilst one at a time a rabbit hops over to them and from the outside of the circle has to try and tag as many people as they can within 10 seconds without stepping over the line.

✦ Each person they tag within that time become captives and so must leave the circle and go over to the prison circle. After the ten seconds that rabbit must return home and another one takes over. At no time must the rabbits put their other foot down, nor can they step over into the circle otherwise they are out of the game.

✦ If before the ten seconds is up the rabbit gets tired then he can hop back home and nominate another rabbit to take his place. The game is over when all the players have been taken prisoners.

✦ For younger children, they could try hopping with both feet together as opposed to just using one foot.

86. Hula-hoop contest

Equipment: Hula hoops

✦ Most schools have hula-hoops in their PE store and this is the ideal game for children to get them out, have fun and get fit at the same time.

✦ When the teacher announces 'go' the players simply hula hoop as long as they can and the winner is the one who manages to keep the hoop spinning for the longest. But if they touch it at anytime with their hands or if the hoop drops then they are out of the game.

87. **Four squared**

Equipment: Chalk; tennis ball

✦ This game is for the playground and perfect for smaller groups to play. Using a piece of chalk mark off a play area approximately two metres square then divide that up again into four equal squares.

✦ A child should stand in each of the four squares, one of them holding a ball. Whoever is holding the ball will bounce it in their square once before tapping it into another players square. Whoever is standing in that square must in turn tap the ball into another players' square provided it has bounced only once in theirs.

✦ Speed is of the essence because if the ball bounces more than once into someone else's square then they are eliminated from the game and either the square is left empty or a new player is rotated to fill that square.

✦ Should your volley go out of the play area before bouncing in the grid then you are out. If your volley goes into a square where there is no player you are also out of the game.

88. Orange

Equipment: Large soft ball

✦ One person is selected as the thrower, the rest of the players gather around him/her.

✦ As the thrower throws the ball into the air he/she must call out the name of someone in the group. This person must then try to catch the ball, and as they do shout out: 'Stop'.

✦ The person who caught the ball must now throw the ball gently trying to hit any player and if a person is hit they are given a letter 'O' from the word Orange.

✦ If the person throwing the ball misses the hit, then they are assigned the letter. The targeted player will be the next one to throw the ball. And once a player has been given all the letters to spell the word 'ORANGE' they are out of the game.

89. **Squat race**

✦ This is a game in which four or more people can join in and is ideal to play outdoors in an open area.

✦ Divide the players up into two teams.

✦ The first players in line have to squat down and grab hold of their ankles. They then have to squat walk to a designated area, turn around and return to the starting line to set the other team members off. They have to tag the next person's foot with their own foot before the next person in line can go.

✦ The winners are the first team to have each member complete the course and return to the beginning.

90. Pretzel relay

✦ This game needs some practice before being played otherwise you will spend more time laughing than actually playing the game.

✦ It's a super game for two or more people and ideal for playing outside on a playing field so if you topple over, which you may very well do, you won't hurt yourself too much.

✦ In order to play you have to stand in a pretzel position and if you haven't a clue what this looks like, the idea is to stand on your left leg, lift your right leg and cross it in front of your left knee, and then cross your arms in front of your body. Don't start the game until you can create the position.

✦ When both players are in position ready, at the command, 'Go', they must hop towards the finishing line and the pretzel that gets there still hopping is the winner!

91. **In and out (1)**

Equipment: Chalk

✦ This is a fun game especially for younger children and will make sure that they are listening to instructions being given. Any number of children can play this game.

✦ The teacher marks out a long line using a piece of chalk. One side of the line represents the river the other side represents the shore.

✦ The idea is for the teacher to call out randomly either in the river or on the shore so the children must listen closely and jump on the side of the line being referred to. If they jump on to the wrong side they are out of the game.

92. **Hop it!**

Equipment: Handkerchief; 2 cones

✦ Great fun for all ages and a game ideally suited for four or more players.

✦ Spilt the players into two teams and give each team a handkerchief.

✦ In order to play, the first player from each team has to carefully balance a handkerchief on his/her foot and then hop to the cone and back again, before the next player goes. If the handkerchief falls or the hopper loses their balance they must return to the start and begin again.

✦ The winning team is the first to complete the task with all team members

93. Traffic Warden

♦ One person from the class is chosen to be the 'Traffic Warden' who stands with their back towards the remainder of the players, approximately 15 metres away.

♦ He/she has to shout out 'Green Light', at which point the children can all begin to move towards him/her. But whenever the Traffic Warden feels like it he/she can call out 'Red Light' and then immediately turn around. On this occasion the players must remain still (rather like Statutes) and the Traffic Warden is allowed to leave their spot and walk around amongst the group for a couple of seconds. If any of the players are caught moving, they are eliminated from the game.

♦ Everyone has to remain perfectly still until the warden returns back to his/her spot turns around and gives the Green Light signal allowing the children to move again. Remember that at any time the Traffic Warden feels like it he/she can call out 'Red Light', turn around and catch a player out.

♦ The aim of the game is for someone to tap the traffic warden on the shoulder and shout out, 'Amber'. They can then take on the role of Traffic Warden and another game can begin. If two or three manage to reach him/her then those three players must play a head to head and whoever wins that round is the winner.

94. **Hoop the balloon**

Equipment: 2 hula hoops; 2 balloons

A fun game to play on a summer afternoon provided there is no wind!

✦　　It involves 10 people, two hula-hoops and two balloons. Both hula-hoops are held by two volunteers some distance from the starting point.

✦　　At the word 'Go' the first player from each team must take the balloon, gently place it between their knees and then run towards the hula-hoop. The tricky part is next when they have to get the balloon into the hoop without using their hands and this isn't as easy as it sounds.

✦　　If they drop the balloon on the way then they have to stop, pick it up and return to where ever they dropped the balloon and start over again.

✦　　Once they manage to get it through the hoop they can then pick up the balloon in their hands and run back as fast as they can to their team, handing the balloon over to the next player who must follow the same procedure.

✦　　The first team to have everyone complete the process successfully and are sitting in a straight line are the winners.

95. Stepping stones

Equipment: White paper; scissors

✦ Two sheets of white paper are needed and this is an ideal game for up to ten players.

✦ Cut a piece of paper in half and hand both pieces to the first player. The object of the game is for each player to reach the end of a course and return but only by stepping on the pieces of paper.

✦ After each step, they place the other piece infront of them to step on. This involves balancing on one foot to pick up the first piece of paper and move it forward. If they stand on the ground and not the paper they have to go back to the start again. Once they reach the end they must do exactly the same for their return to their team.

✦ The winners are the first team in which each member has carried out the procedures and are sitting upright with the two pieces of paper in their hand.

✦ The trick is not to make the space in between the paper too wide otherwise you won't reach and if you make them too close together it will take forever to reach the end.

NOTE: You might need a stone resting on each piece of paper to stop it from blowing away.

96. **Forwards, backwards**

Equipment: Chalk

✦   At least six players are needed for this game.

✦   Divide the players up into two teams of three or more and using some chalk draw a line or mark to determine the turn round point of your course approximately 10 metres away.

✦   Now each player has to follow a sequence of moves to get themselves down the track and back to their team members. The sequence involves the pupils making one hop forward followed by two jumps forward, and one step backwards (or any other sequence you like).

✦   The winning team is the one whose team members have all its players go down the line and back again first. But if anyone forgets what action they should be doing, topples over or hesitates for too long they must return back to the start and begin again.

94

97. Ducts that fly

✦ Loosely based on the game of 'Simon Says' but in this game the players must all imitate the different actions/sounds made by the Caller. If anyone fails to copy him/her they are out of the game. They are also out of the game if the Caller gives a wrong statement, ie cats bark or birds meow, and they make that sound (but everyone can have at least three chances before they are eliminated).

✦ Some samples of true actions:

✧ Dogs bark	Bees buzzzz	Pigs grunt/oink
✧ Cats meow	Horses neigh	Sheep baaa
✧ Snakes hiss	Lions roar	Cockerels cock-a-doodle-do

Some wrong statements:

✧ Horses mooo	Dogs meow	Pigs baaa
✧ Lions bark	Cats roar	Snakes cock a doodle do

98. **Snake awake**

Equipment: *Stopwatch*

✦   One person is chosen to be the snake. He/she must crouch over. Everyone else has to go down on all fours and remain in that position.

✦   The idea is that, as the snake lies 'sleeping' the rest of the players very quietly, on all fours, creep over and very gently place a finger on his/her back. At any time the snake can jump up and shout 'Snake Awake' and rise up from its crouched position. For 30 seconds (teacher may need a stopwatch at this point) the snake can attempt to tag as many people as it is able to before the teacher shouts 'Go to sleep' at which point he/she must return to the crouched position.

✦   Any players who have been tagged are out of the game.

NOTE – it is important that everyone, including the snake, moves only on all fours.

99. Stringing along

Equipment: String

This game is a lot of fun and if players don't concentrate can end up being chaotic.

✦ Divide the class into two teams. Each team has to stand in a circle and give one member of one team a ball of string.

✦ That person then ties one end of the ball of string loosely to one of their fingers and passes the ball to the next person standing beside them, they do the same as the previous person, wrap a piece of string loosely around one of their fingers and then pass it to the next person and so on until the ball of string has been passed around each pupil in the circle several times.

✦ When the string has all been used the excitement begins, as the ball of string must now be returned to the first person by simply rewinding it back. It isn't as easy as it sounds, especially when you are in competition with the other team. Whoever has the string of ball tied up and back to the first team member quickest is the winner.

100. Doctor, Doctor

✦ Select a child to be the Doctor and turn him around so he can't see what's going on with the rest of the children.

✦ Give the rest of the children two minutes to get 'tangled-up'. They must start by holding hands in a line, they can then weave in and out of each other, but mustn't let go of their hands.

✦ Then shout 'Doctor, Doctor' who has to come over and untangle them without them falling over or breaking any links between hands.

101. Murder mystery

✦ It might a good idea to make sure all the children know how to wink before starting this game.

✦ Everyone sits in a circle. One person is selected to be the detective and has to go away until the murderer has been chosen.

✦ The detective walks around the outside of the circle trying to detect who the murderer is.

✦ The murderer should wait until the detective isn't looking and then wink at someone to 'kill' them. The murdered person should wait at least two seconds before moaning and groaning and falling over, dead.

✦ The detective needs to guess who the murderer is. If they guess correctly, they get to swap places with the murderer.

102. Morgan the Monster

✦ Choose one child to be Morgan. You can either pick out children to be Mandy, Jack, Ben, Emma, Sam, Katie and Joe or let Morgan have a choice from all the children in the circle.

✦ Ask all the children except Morgan to sit in a circle. They should have their eyes firmly closed.

All the children chant:
Morgan the monster is out tonight.
Who is the person to get a fright?
Will it be Mandy, will it be Jack?
Will it be Ben, Emma or Sam?
Or will it be Katie or Joe?
Tiptoe quietly across the ground
Ever so quietly without a sound

Boo! (This is said by Morgan only as he grabs the shoulders of a child.)

✦ Meanwhile, Morgan tiptoes very quietly around the outside of the circle and at the point before 'Boo' stops behind a child's back ready to make them jump as he grabs their shoulders and shouts Boo!

103. Sleeping lions

✦ Choose two children to be 'hunters' while all the other children are the 'lions'.

✦ The lions have to lie down on the ground pretending to be asleep.

✦ Meanwhile, the hunters have to move closely in and out of the lions trying to make them move. The hunters may do this by telling jokes, making funny noises, etc but they are not allowed to touch the lions.

✦ Any of the lions who move in any way or giggle must stand up and join the hunters. The winners are the last ones left lying on the ground.

104. Scavenger hunt

✦ Have a good walk around the playing field and playgound looking out for certain items that are in abundance. Make a mental note of these and their whereabouts. (Dandilion leaves or flowers, daisies, feathers, small stones, a twig, etc)

✦ Ask the children to get together in groups of three of four.

✦ Give them a list of items you wish them to collect. The winners are the first group to collect all the items on your list.

105. The farmer's in his den

✦ All the children hold hands in a circle. Ask for a volunteer to be the farmer or select someone yourself. They stand in the middle of the circle.

✦ All the children sing:
> The farmer's in his den,
> The farmer's in his den,
> e, i, daddy oh,
> The farmer's in his den.
>
> The farmer wants a wife,
> The farmer wants a wife,
> e, i, daddy oh,
> The farmer wants a wife.

(At this point the farmer chooses someone from the outer circle and they join him in the middle.)

> The wife wants a child,
> The wife wants a child
> e, i, daddy oh,
> The wife wants a child.

(At this point the wife chooses someone from the outer circle and they join them in the middle.)

> The child wants a dog,
> The child wants a dog,
> e, i, daddy oh,
> The child wants a dog.

(At this point the child chooses someone from the outer circle and they join them in the middle.)

> Everyone pat the dog,
> Everyone pat the dog,
> e, i, daddy oh,
> Everyone pat the dog.

(Everyone from the circle can move in and gently pat the child who has been chosen as the dog.)

106. **Find the Joker**

Equipment: A pack of cards to include both Jokers

✦   Add the Jokers to the pack of cards and sort out enough cards to give one to each of the other children. (Make sure you include both Jokers.)

✦   Tell the children they are going to find the joker amongst them. Hand out the cards. They must not show their cards to anyone or divulge who they are.

✦   Ask the children to mingle together and ask each other questions about themselves. The two children who have the joker cards are not allowed to answer any questions, but must reply with another question.

✦   Once the children come across someone they believe to be the joker they must quietly sit down without letting anyone else know their findings.

✦   The game continues until only the two jokers remain.

107. Higher or lower?

Equipment: A pack of cards

✦ Divide the children into two groups: Team A and Team B. Give each child a card from the pack. They must not show their cards to the other team.

✦ Stand the children in a line opposite each other.

✦ Starting with Team A, shuffle the remaining cards in the pack and let the first player choose one.

✦ Take this card and give it to the first member of the opposing team (Team B) to hold up.

✦ Go back to Team A and ask them as a group to guess whether the secret card held by this person is higher or lower than the one they are showing.

✦ If Team A are correct, the card is shown and they move on to guessing the card of the next player in Team B. Team A have to decide if their card is higher or lower than the previous card.

✦ Team A continues with the game until they are unsuccessful in their guessing. When this happens the roles are reversed. Shuffle the pack again and let the first player from Team B pick a card. Give this card to the first member of Team A and let Team B make the decisions until they are unsuccessful.

✦ The winning team is the one to successfully guess all the opposing team members cards correctly.

108. In and out (2)

✦ Randomly choose 1–3 (depending on how large the group) children from your group to weave in and out.

✦ Ask the rest of the children to form a circle. Ask one child to hold one hand up in the air at an angle and their other hand stretched out horizontally to the side, now ask the children either side of them take up the corresponding position that links up. Hold hands. (See diagram below.)

✦ The children in the circle have to close their eyes while the children chosen have to weave in and out through the circle.

✦ Meanwhile, the children in the circle have to predict when the weaver is about to come under their arms and try to catch them as they do by lowering their arms.

✦ The children must not let go of their partners hand despite the fact they may not be aware when that child might decide to lower their arm to make a catch.

✦ Once they are caught, the weaver has to swop with one of the pair of children who caught him/her.

109. Catch the snake

Equipment: Whistle

✦ Divide the class up into two sides.

✦ Players in each group form a line one behind the other, and place their hands on the hips of the person in front of them.

✦ The person at the front of the line is the head of the snake and they have to try and catch its tail (the last person in the line).

✦ When the teacher blows the whistle, both the heads start to chase after their tail. When it catches it, the head then takes its place and the second in line now becomes the head. This continues until everyone has had a chance at being the head of the snake and the first team to complete this are the winners.

✦ But if, at any point, any team members let go of their partner in front of them they have to start again.

Index

Playground Games

100+ Fun Ideas for ...

... Practicing Modern Foreign Languages

137 tried and tested activities which can be used to develop oracy and literacy skills in any language.

Enjoyable, interactive activities that are guaranteed to get an enthusiastic response from all pupils.

Covers most of the oracy and literacy objectives in the KS2 Framework for languages.

100+ Fun Ideas for ...

... Art Activities

Easy to prepare and enjoyable activities that children will love.

The activites in this book introduce a wide range of art skills and media, and are compatible with the National Curriculum. Activities are suitable for use both in the classroom, at home or in children's clubs. Although primarily aimed at 7–11 year olds, most of the activities can be adapted for younger children.

... Science Investigation

This book contains exciting, fun classroom experiments to help teach scientific investigation.

The activities require a minimum of preparation and only the simplest of science equipment. Each activity provides opportunities for children to develop their skills of scientific enquiry.

The easy-to-use layout, closely matches the statutory and non-statutory guide-lines and schemes of work for Key Stages 1 and 2, will make this an invaluable book for all primary teachers.

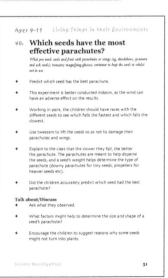

... Transition Times

This book is crammed with stimulating ideas for the awkward, transition times of the day, such as lining-up and answering the register.

The activities have been carefully chosen to ensure pupils work as a team, and develop their self-esteem, physical and mental health, but most importantly, ensure they have fun.

Use these ideas to refresh repetitive routines. If they go smoothly, then the rest of the day will too.

... Wet Playtimes

Provides useful ways to keep KS1 and KS2 pupils occupied during wet playtimes.

Activities have an educational element, where games range from pen and paper games to word games, talking games and even group games.

Games can be easily adapted to suit all primary school children.

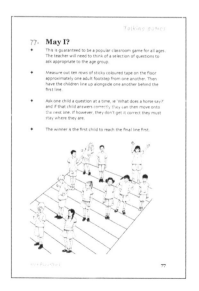

Lightning Source UK Ltd.
Milton Keynes UK
UKOW06f1116230816

281299UK00010B/40/P